ANCIENT GREECE

CITIES & CITIZENS

Jane Shuter

Heinemann Library
Des Plaines, Illinois

© 1999 Reed Educational & Professional Publishing
Published by Heinemann Library,
an imprint of Reed Educational & Professional Publishing,
1350 East Touhy Avenue, Suite 240 West
Des Plaines, IL 60018

03 02 01 00 99
10 9 8 7 6 5 4 3 2 1

Library of Congress Cataloging-in-Publication Data

Shuter, Jane.
    Cities and Citizens / Jane Shuter.
        p.   cm. -- (Ancient Greece)
    Includes bibliographical references and index.
    Summary: Introduces the citizens, government, education, philosophy, religion, and sports of the city states of ancient Greece.
    ISBN 1-57572-738-2
    1. Greece--Civilization-To 146 B.C.--Juvenile literature.
2. Cities and towns, Ancient Greece--Juvenile literature.
[1. Greece--Civilization--To 146 B.C. 2. Greece-
-History, Military. 3. Agriculture--Greece.] I. Title. II. Series:
Ancient Greece (Des Plaines, Ill.)
DF78.S56 1998
938--dc21
                                                    98-7148
                                                       CIP
                                                        AC

Acknowledgments
The Publishers would like to thank the following for permission to reproduce photographs:
American School of Classical Studies, Athens p.8; Ancient Art and Architecture Collection pp. 1,13; R. Sheridan pp. 19, 29; Bildarchiv Preussischer Kulturbesitz pp. 9, 25; C.M. Dixon p. 15; Father R. J. Schoder, S.J. p. 5; Werner Forman Archive p. 21.

Cover photograph reproduced with permission of the British Museum.

Every effort has been made to contact copyright holders of any material reproduced in this book. Any omissions will be rectified in subsequent printings if notice is given to the Publisher.

Any words appearing in the text in bold, **like this**, are explained in the Glossary.

CONTENTS

Ancient Greece

Greece is a country broken up by mountains and the sea. In ancient times, it was very hard to travel around Greece. The Ancient Greeks lived in small groups around a city. They spoke the same language and had the same religion. But they did not see themselves as Greek. They saw themselves as part of a **city-state** (the land controlled by the nearby city). This book looks at how the city-states were run and what they were like to live in.

Timeline

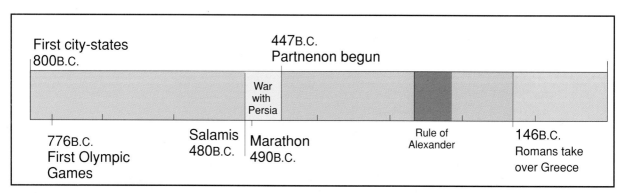

First city-states
800B.C.

447B.C.
Partnenon begun

War with Persia

776B.C.
First Olympic Games

Salamis
480B.C.

Marathon
490B.C.

Rule of Alexander

146B.C.
Romans take over Greece

CITY-STATES

What was a city-state? It was a city and the farmland around it. Some city-states were very small and could have less than a thousand **citizens**. The biggest and most powerful city-states were Athens and Sparta. They had several thousand citizens.

ARISTOTLE, THE ATHENIAN PHILOSOPHER (THINKER), WROTE THAT THE SIZE OF A CITY-STATE WAS IMPORTANT:

You can not have a state of ten citizens. But when you have 100,000, it is no longer a city-state. It has to be big enough to run itself. But it has to be small enough for the citizens to know each other. Otherwise, how can they choose officials?

This photo shows Athens from the air. You can see the Parthenon with its strong walls on the right.

City-states were run in different ways. Some of them were run by kings. Others were run by a small group of powerful men (who came from rich and important families in the city). Other city-states, like Athens, were run by all the **citizens**. Not everyone in Athens had a say in decisions. You had to be a citizen to take part.

ATHENIAN CITIZENS

A citizen had to be a man. He had to be free and not a slave. He had to be the son of an Athenian citizen. He had to be more than 17 years old. Less than one-third of the people of Athens took part in making the decisions.

ALL THE SAME?

City-states were run in different ways, but they all had similar ideas about which people were the most important. **Slaves** were the least important. The most important were rich male citizens. Even in Athens, these were the people most likely to make the decisions. Then came other male citizens. Then came women, children, and foreigners. Women and men lived almost separate lives. Women stayed at home most of the time, in a separate part of the house. They went out as little as possible.

A city **agora**

Athens started as a small **city-state**. It grew to become one of the biggest and most powerful. As it grew, the city became more important and the countryside around it became less important. Athens had too many people to feed from food grown in the nearby farmland. So Athens had to **trade goods**, like pottery and statues, with other countries or Greek **colonies** for food. Athens was near the sea but not beside it. As it grew and traded more and more, the nearby **port** of Piraeus became big and important, too.

People voted on decisions by raising their hands. When more careful counts were needed, **ballots** were used. These ballots were used by people in trials to say if they thought the accused person was guilty or not.

VOTING

Athens was a **democracy** in which all **citizens** voted. Meetings were held about 40 times a year at the Pnyx, a hill near the city. Citizens were rounded up by men with a rope to make sure that they went! A list of things to decide was read aloud. Citizens spoke if they wanted, and then they all voted.

EDUCATION

Education was important in Athens. A good speaker could affect decision making. Boys went to school to learn to read, write, and make speeches. They read books and plays. Many Athenians thought that being a good speaker and thinker was very important, even more important than being a good soldier or hard worker.

Boys went to school for part of the day. They also went to wrestling school so that they were fit when they began to train as soldiers. All men were expected to fight for their city-state.

A GREEK WRITER NAMED PLATO DESCRIBED SCHOOLS IN ATHENS IN ABOUT 390 B.C.:

As soon as boys know their letters and can read well, their teachers give them the works of good poets to read and learn to set the boys a good example of how to behave. Boys also go to wrestling school, so they are fit and able to be brave when they go to war. Sons of wealthy parents begin school at the earliest age and finish their schooling the latest.

Sparta was a very different **city-state** from Athens. They had both begun in a similar way: they had been ruled by kings. Athens went on to have a **democracy**. Sparta was ruled by two kings and a **council** of important men who ran everything.

SPARTAN IDEAS

The most important thing for a Spartan man was to be a good soldier. They trained for this from birth. In Sparta, officials decided whether to let newborn babies live. They chose only the strongest boys and girls. When a boy was seven, he left home to be brought up with other boys. He lived with other soldiers until he was 30. If he married, he had a house for his wife and visited from time to time. After he became 30, he could live at home.

PLUTARCH, A WRITER, DESCRIBED SCHOOLS IN SPARTA:

They learned reading and writing for basic needs, but the rest of their education was to make them brave, well-disciplined soldiers. Their bodies were tough, unused to baths and lotions.

SPARTAN WOMEN

Spartan girls were expected to be very fit, unlike girls in other city-states. The usual women's jobs of spinning and weaving were considered not to be active enough for Spartan women. They were encouraged to be active and healthy so that they would have strong, healthy babies.

A bronze figure of a Spartan girl running.

Many important thinkers were Greek. Some of their ideas are still talked about today. Most of them believed that thinking ideas through and proving them was enough. Only a few of them made useful inventions. One of these was Archimedes. He is interesting because he was so unusual.

ARCHIMEDES

Archimedes was born in about 287 B.C. He invented a way of lifting water from rivers so that it could be used to water farmland. He calculated that by using a lever that was properly balanced, you could move very heavy loads. He proved it by **launching** the biggest ship he could find, the *Syracusa*. It was fully loaded and weighed about 1,984 tons. By using a complicated system of levers and pulleys, Archimedes launched it from a ramp all by himself.

Archimedes designed several weapons to help the Greeks fight the Romans. He was killed in 212 B.C., when the Romans captured his city. There is a story that he was killed by a Roman soldier for refusing to be arrested until he had finished an experiment he was working on!

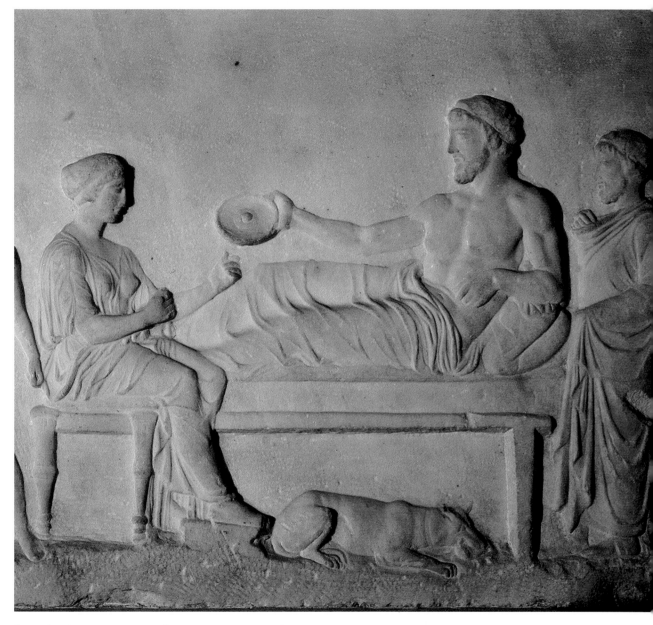

People disapproved of some thinkers. One example is Socrates, who taught young men to question their elders. He was accused of corrupting the young men and was sentenced to death. This frieze shows him drinking the poisoned wine given to kill him.

Writing was important to the Ancient Greeks. Even the Spartans believed that everyone needed to learn to read and write. Much of what we know about the Greeks, we know because of the books and plays they wrote. Many of these have survived and we can read them today.

THE ALPHABET

Our word "alphabet" comes from the first two letters of the Greek alphabet "alpha" and "beta." Our alphabet has been based on the Greek alphabet. We do not share all the letters of the alphabet because English does not make the same sounds as Greek.

WHAT DID THEY WRITE ON?

The earliest Greeks carved writing onto stones or scratched it onto metal or pieces of pottery. Boys practiced writing at school on wax, so mistakes could be smoothed out. Later, they used paper scrolls and books. The paper was made from the stalks of papyrus reeds. Most of the paper came from Egypt.

This example of Greek writing, dating from before 500 B.C.
was scratched onto lead, which could be used because it is
a reasonably soft metal.

Temples were the grandest and most important parts of any city. They were also built the best. They are the buildings most likely to have survived until today. A temple was the home of the god or goddess it was dedicated to. Only **priests** and **priestesses** could go into a temple. Ordinary people did not go inside. The **religious ceremonies** and the **sacrifices** were held outside.

PRIESTS AND PRIESTESSES

Priests and priestesses were important people. They ran the temples and made the sacrifices to the many gods and goddesses of Ancient Greece. The Greeks believed in many different gods and goddesses who could come to earth and interfere in the lives of ordinary people. So the gods had to be kept happy with prayers, sacrifices, and religious ceremonies. Greeks believed their gods and goddesses behaved like people and could get into fights, fall in love, and become jealous. People could pray to the gods at home, but they also had to go to the temples for the big religious ceremonies.

A procession to a temple

Almost every Greek city had at least one theater. Many of them have survived, so people are able to study them today. Theater performances were part of **religious ceremonies**. They only happened a few times in a year. You could not go to the theater every day.

The playwrights who wrote the plays used stories that people knew. They did not make up new stories. Many plays were written especially for a ceremony. Three were chosen and performed. The audiences voted for the one they liked best.

WHO ACTED?

All the actors were men. Because they were a long way from many of the people in the audience, the actors wore heavy masks made of linen, cork, or wood. These masks clearly showed the audience what the actor was supposed to be—a man or a woman, young or old. Some masks had a happy face on one side and a sad one on the other, so an actor could change his feelings by turning the mask around.

The Greek theater at Syracuse in Sicily

WHO WENT?

Men wrote plays and went to the theater. Some historians think women did not go to the theater because they had to stay at home and keep away from the men. Other historians say that women went to **religious festivals** and plays were part of these, so they may have gone to the theater. We have no proof either way.

As plays became more complicated, two kinds developed. Tragedies retold myths, which were usually stories in which the most important character has an unhappy end. They warned against arguing with the gods or getting too proud or important. Comedies were funny. They made fun of all kinds of people. Their characters and storylines were more ordinary. They were often rude, as well as funny. There were often dwarfs acting as servants in the comedies. They were the earliest kind of circus clown.

MENANDER

A playwright named Menander was born in about 341 B.C. He lived in Athens and came from an important family. He wrote mostly comedies. His plays won first prize several times. Only one whole play has survived. We know he wrote over one hundred plays because other writers talk about them in their plays and books. He died in about 291 B.C.

A carving of Menander (sitting down) looking at actors' masks. He is holding a mask of a young man. Masks for an older man and a woman are on the table beside him.

What do we know about Ancient Greek actors? Some actors became well known as tragic or comic actors. But they were not famous in the way actors are today. First, no one saw their faces. They wore masks to act. Second, they only acted when there was a **religious festival**. Third, the playwright and his ideas, not the actors, were what was seen as important.

THE CHORUS

Plays were either spoken or sung in rhyme. The actors stood on a stage behind the **orchestra**. The orchestra was not the musicians! It was a big space in the center of the theater where the chorus stood. There were about 15 people in the chorus. They all spoke together. They told the story and made comments on what was happening. They also danced and sang. The actors got the big speeches. Only three actors were on the stage at any time. But they could play more than one part.

A play being performed in a Greek theatre.
The chorus are in the orchestra on the right.

The Ancient Greeks held the first Olympic Games. All the **city-states** in Greece joined. If any of them were fighting each other, they stopped to let each other travel to get to the Olympics. The Olympics were held every four years like they are now. But they were different in several ways.

A RELIGIOUS FESTIVAL

The Olympics were part of a **religious festival** held at Olympia. It was held in honor of the most important of the gods, Zeus. They began with religious **processions** and **sacrifices**. **Religious ceremonies** took up two and a half of the five days of the Olympics.

MEN ONLY

Only men could take part in the Olympics. The athletes competed naked. Women could not watch. The punishment for women caught watching was to be thrown off a cliff! Women had their own games, which were held at the same time but in a different part of Olympia. They were held in honor of Zeus' wife, Hera.

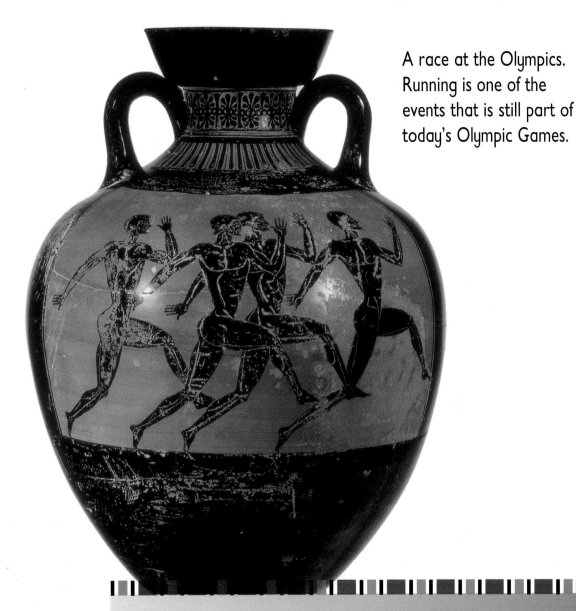

A race at the Olympics. Running is one of the events that is still part of today's Olympic Games.

Aren't you burned by the sun? Aren't you crowded and tight packed? Aren't the washing facilities bad? Aren't you soaked to the skin when it rains? Don't you get more than enough noise and shouting and other unpleasantness? Yet, you put up with all of this because it is such a marvelous spectacle.

All Greeks, not just athletes, were expected to keep fit. **City-states** could call on their **citizens** to fight at any time. So keeping fit was important in case you had to go to war. Doctors said keeping fit kept you healthy. All Greek towns had at least one **gymnasium**, a place where men could go to exercise.

AT THE GYMNASIUM

A gymnasium was not a building as it is today. It was an open park with trees and grass. There were running tracks marked off and sandy areas for jumping, boxing, and wrestling. There were also changing rooms and places to wash.

NOT JUST EXERCISE

Men went to a gymnasium to chat, not just to exercise. In Athens' gymnasium, there was a lot of teaching, too. Famous thinkers taught small groups. By 250 B.C., some gymnasiums even had libraries and lecture rooms.

EVIDENCE FROM THE TIME

We know about the important buildings like **temples** in cities because they have survived and can be studied.

NEW EVIDENCE

Archaeologists have excavated parts of some Greek cities. There is not much left to study. Ordinary houses made from mud brick have crumbled away. Also, some cities like Athens have been lived in since ancient times. Modern homes cover the ancient city.

A DESCRIPTION OF ATHENS WRITTEN IN ABOUT 320 B.C.:

The city is dry and dusty with a bad water supply. The streets are badly planned because the city is so old. Many of the houses need repairs, and there are not many large ones. A stranger would be very surprised that this was the famous city of Athens. But the public buildings are magnificent. The theater is large and beautiful. The Temple to Athena, called the Parthenon, is clearly visible from a long way off. Anyone who sees it will be amazed by it.

DELOS

Archaeologists excavated the Greek town on the island of Delos. This town had been deserted and not built over, so the stone bases of the houses can be studied. The island is only 3.1 miles (5 kilometers) by 0.8 miles (1.3 kilometers) and has no fresh water supply. But it was an important trading city in Ancient Greek times and was taken over and used by the Romans. It was famous for being where the god Apollo was born, and people visited to pray at his **temple** there.

GLOSSARY

agora an open space often near the center of a town with public buildings and shops. It was often used as a meeting place.

archaeologists people who dig up and study things left behind from past times

ballots discs used by juries to vote

citizens people who are born in a city to parents who were citizens. A citizen had rights in their own city that they would not have in another one.

city-state a city and the surrounding land it controls

colonies places set up in one country by people from another country

council a group of people chosen to give advice

democracy running the country by letting the citizens make the decisions

goods things that are made, bought, and sold

gymnasium a place where Greek men went to exercise in the open air

launching moving a ship from a dry place on land into the sea

orchestra the main central part of the theater where the chorus chanted, sang, and danced

port a town by the sea where ships can land

priest a person who works in a temple and serves a god or goddess

priestesses a female priest

procession a march from one place to another that follows a set route

religious ceremonies special times when people go to one place to pray to a god or goddess

religious festival several days of religious ceremonies usually held every year

sacrifices something given to a god or goddess as a gift. If the sacrifice was a living thing, it was killed before it was given.

slaves people who are treated by their owners as property. They can be bought and sold and are not free to leave.

temple a place where gods and goddesses are worshiped

trade this has two meanings: a job, for example, "Shoemaking is his trade."; or selling or swapping goods, for example, "Greeks traded oil for grain."

INDEX

MORE BOOKS TO READ

Chelepi, Chris. *Growing up in Ancient Greece.* Mahwah, NJ: Troll
    Communications L.L.C. 1997.

Nardo, Don. *Life in Ancient Greece.* San Diego, CA: Lucent
    Books. 1996.

Pearson, Anne. *Everyday Life in Ancient Greece.* Franklin Watts,
    Inc. 1994.

Vernerey, Denise. *The Ancient Greeks: In the Land of the Gods.*
    Brookfield, CT: Millbrook Press, Inc. 1997.